We Have to Stop It

Walter Smelt III

"Building Direct Democracy in an Atlanta Forest " and "Boston Area Students Against Genocide " originally appeared in *Counterpunch*

ISBN: 978-1-967022-17-5

Fomite
Burlingon, VT
fomitepress.com

The thing we have to do is stop it. This is what people who opposed the evil of slavery knew. This is what people who opposed the lynchings of black citizens knew. This is what those who opposed the genocide of the Vietnamese by US forces knew. This is what the people who oppose the genocide of the Palestinians in Gaza and other parts of Palestine know. This is what the people opposing the kidnappings of workers, students and others know. This is what we all know, and but for our fear of losing our comforts or our status, we should be doing something to stop the intensifying repression we see around us.

Some of those reading this will know that the repression is not new. Indeed, it is an important part of how nations and societies are ruled. In the case of the United States (and most of the rest of the world) the majority of us are ruled by those who control the world's wealth. As that wealth has accumulated among an ever smaller percentage of the population, the repression has intensified. The increasing numbers of authoritarian regimes is but the most obvious representation of this. These regimes deserve our disrespect and protest. Then again, so do many of their predecessors. These fascists and autocrats were not birthed in a vacuum, nor did the rise to power without financial and logistical support from those whose interests they serve—the wealthy and their networks. From Trump to Netanyahu and beyond, these rulers are in power because the wealth they protect requires a more brutal policing of those whose wealth has been stolen.

Among the latter group we can find the working and the unemployed poor, the indigenous and the non-white skinned, the migrant and the refugee; those whose land has been stolen, their children slaughtered or refused, their lives regulated by police and surveillance of every imaginable kind. We also find the prisoner and the detainee, the deported and the unhoused. If we continue our search, if we gaze deeper, we will discover that the situation so many of these folks find themselves in is related to the economics that define to much of everyone's lives. It's an economics that determines in all too many ways the lives we each will live; how we will earn a living, where we will live and the stability of these lives. The poorer one is usually determines all of these and more. When the demands of the billionaire class create upheaval that results in anger from those whose lives they have upended, the response of the rulers is to intensify repression. If one is honest with themselves and acknowledges that, while the faces at the top change, the rule of capital does not. Upon accepting this fact, it becomes easier to see that although trumpism is trending towards greater repression than before, repression has increased with each successive presidential administration in the US.

Despite a very temporary lull in this trend in the years immediately following the resignation of Richard Nixon in 1974 and the public discussion of police state operations like COINTELPRO, history tells us that by the time Bill Clinton pushed through his omnibus crime bill in 1993 (with the support of most Democrats and Republicans including Bernie Sanders and Joe Biden), the repressive organs of the US government had become more sophisticated, insidious and more ubiquitous. The combination of advances in computer technology, a drastic increase in police forces and the militarization of those forces are just a few of he reasons this occurred.

Since the 1990s, this repressive apparatus has only intensified, from George W. Bush's roundups of Muslim and other immigrants after the events known as 9-11 to Barack Obama's signing the 2011 National Defense Authorization Act (NDAA) that codified indefinite military detention without charge or trial into law for the first time in American history. It is but a small step to the Muslim bans of Donald Trump's first administration and Joe Biden's detention of hundreds of thousands of migrants during his four years in the White House. As I write this at the end of April 2025, the news tells me of a judge arrested for making sure an immigrant in her court received due process—a right afforded to everyone who lives in the United States. In other words, the judge was arrested and charged by the US "Department of Justice" for upholding the law—a law the trumpists disagree with. The reaction to this arrest has been fairly muted so far, especially considering its implications. Does this verify the idea that the rulers in the court of capital, no matter what their party identification, agree with the repressive measures being implemented against those who disagree with the power in Washington, DC?

This pamphlet or tract, if you will, includes two reports/essays about the nature of repression in contemporary USA. Written by poet and college professor Walter Smelt, they look at two movements that became much more public during the Biden administration than at any time prior to those four years. The first piece discusses the policing academy known as Cop City in Atlanta. The second one discusses the encampments protesting the US-Israeli genocide of Palestinians in Gaza in 2024. Both essays reveal a common thread—the concern for humanity expressed in the protests and Smelt's discussion of them. It is a concern we must broadcast before it becomes meaningless.

-Ron Jacobs

Building Direct Democracy in an Atlanta Forest

On the edge of a forest just south of Atlanta, I sat in the shade of a gazebo on a hot day in May of 2022, speaking to two activists. Parkgoers sweated in their short sleeves as they strolled past a concrete wall, on which graffiti said DEFEND THE FOREST over a fist sprouting up from roots like a squat tree trunk.

The two activists, along with many others, had taken the graffiti's message to heart and were trying to stop large tracts of the South River Forest from being developed into a privately owned soundstage and a sprawling training center for police, dubbed Cop City. Since that day, the gazebo has been ripped apart by heavy equipment, eighteen activists have been charged with "domestic terrorism," and one forest defender has been shot and killed by police.

Much has been said on the American left about the movement to defend the South Atlanta Forest, for good reason. For one thing, it is a coalition of individuals and organizations brought together by disparate concerns, especially about the environment (and environmental racism) and policing. For another, it has employed a diversity of tactics (from children's marches to Molotov cocktails) without members of the movement scrambling to distance themselves from one another over these differences. It is also notable that one tactic, Earth First!-style tree-sits to prevent clearing, is being used in an unusually urban context. Activists have also mounted pressure campaigns against subcontractors hired by the main contractor, Brasfield & Gorrie, slowing down the project by creating financial disincentives to work on it.

One of the movement's most remarkable features, however, is its insistence on treating public land as truly public—held in common by the people. Activists have not only camped out in the forest to prevent clearing but have continually held community events, inviting people from Atlanta and elsewhere to enjoy themselves in a green space, to see the land's potential. These events have included barbecues and weekly dinners, concerts and raves, puppet shows, art shows, and skill shares where participants learn about plant identification, yoga, herbal medicine, and more. When a friend of mine went to Atlanta for work last August, I suggested he stop by the forest. He did and stumbled on a concert being given by one of his favorite singers, Raury, amid the trees. The forest has even hosted ritual events from different traditions, such as a witches' bonfire and Sukkot and Shabbat ceremonies.

The fight to defend the forest has thus been grounded in a positive vision of people in active relationship with the land, in a shared enjoyment of public space—in democracy that grows from the ground up—even as elected officials, the wealthy, and the police have insisted on an alternative vision: one of unilateral decisions, prosecutorial intimidation, and brute force.

The details are complicated (see this timeline) but involve a public-private land swap, environmental concerns, and residents shut out of the decision-making process. The Atlanta Police Foundation, a nonprofit supporter of the Atlanta Police Department with big corporate donors, wants to build a new $90-million police training facility on land owned by the city of Atlanta but lying outside city limits, in unincorporated Dekalb County. This means the largely Black residents who would be most affected did not elect those with the power to approve the military-grade facility, which was initially planned to include shooting ranges, an area for explosive tests, burn buildings for firefighters, and a mock city for practicing police raids (giving rise to the Cop City nickname). A related land swap transferred nearby Intrenchment Creek Park (site of the gazebo) to a private company, Blackhall Studios, to build a soundstage on—even though the parcel was given to Dekalb County in 2003 on condition it remain a park forever.

The environmental impacts of the proposed development helped galvanize initial opposition. The city-owned property that would hold the facility had been earmarked by Atlanta itself in a 2017 document as integral to plans to create "a massive urban park." Environmentalists argued that destroying woodland would worsen flooding and raise temperatures—a shortsighted move in a changing climate. But local politicians said the facility was needed to boost local police morale and retention after the George Floyd uprising of 2020 (fueled in Atlanta by the killing of Rayshard Brooks as he ran away from police). When a virtual city council meeting was held in September 2021 to hear from residents about Cop City, most who called in seemed unimpressed by the morale argument. Between environmental concerns and locals' worries about noise and other disruptions, 17 hours of public comment was recorded—opposed to the project by a two-to-one ratio. Calls supporting Cop City came mostly from police officers and residents of wealthier, whiter neighborhoods. Despite overwhelming opposition from the affected locals, the city council voted to approve the project.

Opponents of Cop City had used all the city-approved means at their disposal—public comments, courts, peaceful protests—to make their voices heard. Whether or not they were heard, they certainly weren't heeded. Instead, city councilors went ahead with a project developed by the unaccountable Atlanta Police Foundation and funded by $30 million of taxpayer money, with the remaining $60 million coming from corporate sponsors such as Delta Airlines, Wells Fargo, UPS, the Home Depot— even my beloved Waffle House. The failure of the "democratic process" to change a top-down decree to build Cop City on public land with public money is seldom mentioned by local officials expressing shock that opposition started to take less legal, and more militant, forms.

Ryan Millsap, who talked the city into a land swap to build a huge soundstage on Intrenchment Creek Park, then sold his film company but retained ownership of the property. He has so far declined to explain any new plans for its development, but in July he blocked public access to the park and in December he demolished the gazebo, though the terms of the swap required public access be maintained until equivalent facilities were built elsewhere. Police did nothing to stop this apparent flouting of the agreement, but activists took matters into their own hands, blocking and torching heavy equipment—and Millsap's pickup.

The veneer of a democratic civic process has gotten vanishingly thin as one member after another of the citizen's advisory committee for the project has defected from the Cop City consensus. One member, an environmental engineer, was taken off the board after voicing criticism of the project. Another has filed an appeal of the land-disturbance permit for construction. Still another resigned after the tragic climax of the government's efforts to impose their will on the land: the killing of a protester by police.

Before that day, police had raided the activists' camp repeatedly, slashing tents and wrecking other equipment. (This kind of property damage never seems to merit outcry from officials, no more than when it's inflicted on homeless encampments elsewhere.) Raids had been met with thrown stones and fireworks; one activist told me last year that they had succeeded in making "police afraid of the forest," an unpredictable space full of shadowy opponents.

Nonetheless, protesters were arrested during these raids, some later charged with "domestic terrorism" under a vague state law passed after Dylann Roof's mass murder of Black churchgoers. The law is not being used against white supremacist murderers but apparently to intimidate activists, since no more concrete charges have been brought against the so-called terrorists than trespassing. (This parallels the aggressive prosecution of environmentalist Jessica Reznicek, whose sabotage of pipeline equipment resulted in an eight-year sentence with a domestic terrorism enhancement.)

Then, on January 18, a multi-agency police force raided the woods and again began slashing tents and rounding up activists. According to the Georgia Bureau of Investigation, a forest defender named Manuel Teran (called Tortuguita by their comrades) disobeyed orders and shot at Georgia State Patrol officers, who returned fire. An autopsy later showed Tortuguita was shot at least a dozen times. One officer went to the hospital with a bullet wound and recovered.

Authorities said no body cameras recorded the killing, but eventually released videos that caught the sound of gunfire from farther away. On camera, a heavily armored police officer notes the shots sounded like suppressed fire. This would be consistent with the guns carried by the Georgia State Patrol but not the recovered firearm said to belong to Tortuguita. The wearer of the body cam even says, "Man, you fucked your own officer up."

Exactly what happened may never be known to those not on the scene, but activists have loudly doubted that Tortuguita—on record as an advocate of nonviolence—would have fired on officers. Law enforcement in the area does not have a sterling reputation for honesty; in a notorious 2006 case, Atlanta police executed a no-knock raid of a 92-year-old woman's home, who in her surprise fired above the home invaders' heads. They shot her to death and planted drugs in the house, claiming she had hit them when they had, in fact, shot each other.

How to interpret Tortuguita's killing is the most emotionally charged of many disputes over meaning in Atlanta. The core questions are: who does the land belong to, and who belongs to the land? Activists emphasize that the area's Black residents were shut out of the decision-making process, and that the land's history has long been tied to oppression. For much of the 20th century, the city-owned property was a prison farm run on unfree, racialized labor. It is very possible the site holds unmarked graves from this period. Long before, the area belonged to the Muscogee Creek people, until they were pushed off the land by white settlers. Activists have connected the present fight to this original injustice, and in November 2021 Muscogee people from Oklahoma returned to perform a stomp ceremony on their ancestral land for the first time in centuries. Forest defenders refer to the woods by its Muscogee name, the Weelaunee Forest.

Meanwhile, current Atlanta mayor Andre Dickens has disputed that the area at issue even is a forest, saying, "This is Atlanta, and we know forests. This facility would not be built over a forest." This desperate definitional gambit seems to rest on the idea that the woods on the prison farm site are relatively new, and composed less of hardwood trees than of softwoods and "invasive species"—as if no nonnative species could form part of a healthy ecosystem.

In a curious way, this emphasis on invasive species mirrors another piece of the official narrative about Weelaunee Forest: that the forest defenders are mostly "outside agitators," stirring up trouble that Georgians want no part of. This is a very old trope, as liberal Northerners who came down during the civil rights struggle were often called the same thing. Cop City opponents have pointed out the hypocrisy of this messaging, since the Atlanta Police Department itself estimates that 43% of trainees at the new facility will come from out of state. I would add that the business-friendly government of Atlanta has never been at pains to stop the free flow of capital from beyond Georgia, or of visitors spending tourist dollars. It is only outsiders concerned with the environment who are suspect—apparently the wrong shade of green.

Do new woods growing over old injustices constitute a forest? To whom does that forest belong—the public, elected officials, the officials' corporate sponsors? Or perhaps to itself, its trees, water, animals? What property is sacrosanct—trees and paths on public land, a gazebo shading parkgoers, or construction equipment and the windows of the Atlanta Police Foundation (smashed during a march after Tortuguita's killing)? And who is a terrorist? A smiling 26-year-old who tried to protect the land, or the paramilitary force that invaded a camp with guns drawn?

It remains to be seen how these questions will be answered in Atlanta, but the answers concern us all. The problem of militarized police killing with impunity is an American problem. So is the struggle for democratic ownership of the commons against developers' and corporations' priorities (profits, and the police to protect them). So is the need for green space in a warming world, space that can cool our cities and stave off flooding, space that will renew us and remind us where we come from.

For now, city officials seem to be on the defensive. On January 31, 2023 they announced new "compromises" around the project's environmental protections, even though, effectively, nothing had changed. On February 7th, Mayor Andre Dickens lost his cool repeatedly at a meeting with Georgia HBCU students who asked hard questions and sometimes booed him—though he never went so far as to accuse them of being outside agitators. The powers-that-be may have overplayed their hand—trying to quash a movement, they instead created a martyr. After Tortuguita's killing, Atlanta's public radio station WABE held a conversation about Cop City between one liberal and one conservative pundit, who agreed on the bottom line: Cop City would be built as the conclusion to a "democratic process." As the Republican strategist said, "It's not like this is some right-wing administration in Atlanta that's foisting this on this Democratic city. This is a Democratic-led city making this decision."

What is increasingly obvious to people everywhere is that the party making decisions is often immaterial, as neither works for the people. Cop City is spilling the open secret of who counts in this system of governance: police over other citizens, and corporations most of all.

Driving out of Atlanta the day after Tortuguita was killed, I passed the entrance to Doll's Head Trail, a quirky recent addition to the larger South Atlanta Forest. The trail is dotted with dolls that have been arranged with other discarded objects to make a creepy-cute public art project, started by one underemployed carpenter and grown with the help of other volunteers. Though its makers might not characterize it this way, the trail is anarchism in action: individuals taking it upon themselves to act without asking permission; idiosyncratic visions joining to make the commons better for all. It's an organic process that mirrors nature's opportunistic growth and mutualism, one that can't be understood by a top-down government or the extractive logic of capital, and it's sending down new roots in the Atlanta forest.

Boston Area Students Against Genocide

When I strolled into Harvard Yard around
6:00pm on Friday, a Shabbat service was taking
place in the student encampment for Palestine.
Dozens of young people were seated in a large
circle on the lawn, many wearing keffiyehs, a
few wearing kippahs, and at least one wearing
both. A guitar player strummed and led the
circle in a Yiddish song while campers nearby
talked in small groups, or stared at laptops,
perhaps preparing for finals. Three police
SUVs were parked in sight of the camp on
the centuries-old Yard, and a keffiyeh was tied
around the sculpted head of the university's
namesake, John Harvard.

The encampment—or "the Liberated
Zone," as a big banner proclaimed it—now
consisted of more than 40 tents. It had grown
since Wednesday, when it was assembled by
surprise during a noon rally on the last day of
classes. Video of the moment shows students
suddenly dashing onto the grass with backpacks,
tarps, and bags to begin erecting tents while
supporters cheer.

I had come to observe the camp and
speak with Lea Kayali, a campus organizer and
Palestinian American in her third year at Harvard
Law School. Her family is from Jaffa and the

West Bank, and the bombardment of Gaza has hit her hard. "I wake up and read the names of the dead," she said, "the places that have been destroyed. Each headline is more gutting than the last." Even Kayali's cousins in the West Bank, whom she said don't leave their houses for fear of being attacked by settlers or arrested, always remind her: "Keep eyes on Gaza."

Though the devastation of Gaza can feel distant in the US, according to Kayali it is not. This is the point being made by student protesters at Harvard, Columbia University (where an encampment, and its police suppression, first made headlines), and other campuses across the country. Student demands include disclosure of investments in Israeli companies and others profiting from the attack on and occupation of Palestine, and divestment from those companies.

Kayali has been heartened by the enthusiasm of students new to the movement. "It's been activating for many on campus," she said, emphasizing the collective labor the camp requires. Students coordinate food and organize political programming, like a teach-in on the history of student activism. The camp, she said, "is an exemplar of community care, mutual aid."

The moment the tents popped up, Kayali said, "the only sound you could hear was cheering. And this was from students who were just walking through the Yard!" Arabic students began to dance the dabke, a Palestinian folk dance, in a huge circle after the tents were raised. "Seeing a revolutionary joy that has really been absent the last seven months gave me more assurance that we can build the world we want," she added. (When I left her, Kayali got up to help a couple of Black students practicing the steps to the dabke.)

Another inspiring moment for Kayali came Thursday during a visit to the encampment at Northeastern University, across the Charles River in Boston. There, the camp was encircled by a large ring of Boston police in riot gear, with helmets and zip tie handcuffs. But the activists stood in a smaller circle around the tents, linking arms and standing their ground. For about 20 minutes, she said, there was an intense stand-off. And then the police backed off.

Kayali's visit to Northeastern typifies the supportive relationship among area encampments, as many student activists communicate across campuses. For instance, a speaker at a pro-Palestinian rally this week at Berklee College of Music mentioned spending time at the Emerson College encampment before it was violently broken up by police and over 100 arrests were made. That Berklee rally ended with a march to join the Northeastern encampment.

Though the police pressure on Northeastern dissipated Thursday without mass arrests, early Saturday morning the school administration followed through on their threats to break up the camp. This time, Northeastern police, the Boston police, and Massachusetts state troopers detained over 100 students, arresting those who could not or would not produce Northeastern IDs. The tents and other camp equipment were thrown into moving trucks.

I saw one of these moving trucks leaving as I entered the Northeastern campus Saturday morning around 10am. Where the camp had been was an unbroken green expanse, empty of tents and students, surrounded by metal barricades. Nearby, a group of students faced some police officers and chanted "Israel bombs, NEU pays! How many kids did you kill today?"

A Northeastern student on the scene, senior Sarah Barber, told me that Northeastern's ties to the defense industry, particularly Raytheon, had long been a subject of debate on campus. Even when she was a freshman, there were posters in common spaces that said "Pull out of Raytheon." In fact, in 2023 the Student Government Association voted to call on school administration to end contracts with private military companies.

Barber said she was sympathetic to the camp, but also worried that if she joined, the university might withhold her diploma. She saw many on campus who were supportive of the encampment and the Palestinian cause, but others were hostile, and tempers sometimes ran high. Barber said, "I once walked by a girl in a hijab being screamed at by people. I asked if she was okay, and she said, 'They just started screaming at me about Gaza.'"

The administration's excuse for breaking up the camp was that it included "professional protesters" from outside, and that antisemitic chants had been heard, including "Kill the Jews." But as another pro-Palestinian student on the scene, Alina Caudle, pointed out, that phrase was actually yelled by a counter-protester Friday night at the camp. In video of the incident, a young man draped in an Israeli flag shouted, "Kill the Jews! Anybody on board? That's what you chanted for!" Pro-Palestinian students can then be heard shouting him down.

I stopped by the MIT encampment on Sunday, a warm spring day. Students talked, snacked, worked on laptops, or spoke to visitors. While I was there, a couple of mothers from Lexington came to ask how they could help, and a high school student took some pictures. Seated on a lawn chair in the sun, I spoke for over an hour to Zeno (who uses just his last name), a graduate student at MIT's Sloan School of Management—Netanyahu's alma mater.

Zeno, a former captain in the Air Force, had been active in the Black Graduate Students Association (BGSA) before October 7. He explained, "We were doing a lot of group studies on different liberation movements. My family's Black American and my mother's Puerto Rican—through that side there's indigenous Taino—so being Black and indigenous, I know oppressed populations when I see them."

Groups that Zeno organized with demonstrated for a ceasefire and held a teach-in about Black and Palestinian solidarity. MIT Graduates for Palestine began researching and publishing about MIT's ties to the Israeli Ministry of Defense. Student groups also created referenda calling for an immediate ceasefire and an end to MIT's "special relationship" with the Israeli ministry; a vote by MIT undergraduates resulted in 63% support for such a resolution, and MIT graduate students voted 70% in favor.

"One of the more concerning pieces of research," Zeno said, "involves autonomous robotic swarms. Imagine quadcopter drones being AI-driven rather than piloted, and imagine if they could swarm together. AI built by Zionists—how dangerous would that be? Sci-fi kind of stuff."

When the police cracked down at Columbia, MIT students quickly came together on the night of Sunday, April 21, to set up tents. Zeno said it garnered a lot of support from other students and faculty.

He explained, "It's a hearts and minds campaign—but first hearts. When you put yourself on the line, risking arrest, risking your career, that inspires people. We get more and more courage. Someone might say, 'I was nervous about what my lab might think of me,' but now they're spending the night out here. So every day we're growing the community."

Zeno understands the risks better than many. When the Emerson College encampment was threatened late Wednesday night, he and about ten other MIT students answered a call for support and crossed the Charles River to join the Emerson activists.

Zeno said, "The state troopers pulled up with lots of cars, zip ties, face shields, very militarized." The MIT students were chanting when confronted by a policeman, who said they wouldn't be arrested if they left immediately. "We didn't reply except to start chanting 'Free Palestine,' at which point the cops got… agitated."

He said his face was slammed against the wall, and then he was slammed against the hood of the police car. "I told the cop, I'm a disabled veteran, I have an autoimmune disorder that makes my fascia tight, so you have to be careful how you're cuffing me. My arms don't move that far up my back! But he kept trying to force them farther up." According to Zeno, his friend, a Black Muslim, had his head banged on the ground, resulting in a concussion. Despite this and other injuries to protesters, police initially claimed the only injuries were to officers.

Just as the crackdown at Columbia begot more college encampments, though, this police violence only increased students' solidarity. Zeno described how, as he was being cuffed with his face against the hood of the car, he was looking into the eyes of another MIT student being cuffed on the other side of the car. Laughing, he said, "She was newer to the camp, I hadn't even talked to her yet, but we trauma-bonded."

When I ask about how solidarity with Palestine connects to other causes, Zeno warms to his topic. He talks about white supremacy, corruption in the military, the two-party system, the working class, climate change, while a student in a colorful crocheted kipah with a Star of David necklace steps closer and starts nodding. "I see vets unhoused and people walking over them! This is a full-on dystopia and this is not how society is supposed to function. And then I come here and see people helping each other, pooling their resources, and not to add to their 401k."

He pauses. "We could be so much better. We have the imagination to build a better society, and it's people like this administration who can't see it."

His words reminded me of the Shabbat service I'd heard two days before at Harvard. Someone was unfolding the passage where the prophet Moses asks to see the face of God. They said, "Moses, after fleeing persecution, dares to ask for the unimaginable. When I think of my ancestors, I think of his courage in asking this. But the difference is, what we are asking for is not unimaginable. We are imagining it here together as one. Shabbat Shalom!"

In the background, I could see Kayali still practicing the dabke. She had been joined by a couple more people who jumped and wheeled together, the circle widening as I walked away.

Afterword

Looking back at these two pieces from the perspective of June 2025, when I'm writing this, could make for disappointment. Hasn't Cop City been built? (It has.) Weren't the encampments dismantled, whether by police or the students themselves? (They were.)

But rereading them I find more reason for optimism. Though some Stop Cop City activists face criminal charges, and some student activists have been harshly sanctioned by their universities, many remain active in these or other fights. They have not forgotten the need to struggle. They are learning from both victories and defeats. And they are connecting the dots.

Last night at an independent theater, I saw the documentary The Encampments, about pro-Palestinian campus protests. (One shot shows a tent with a sign on it that says "Stop Cop City"—a message I also saw at the Harvard and MIT encampments.) The film prominently features Mahmoud Khalil, a graduate student who negotiated with the Columbia administration on behalf of activists and who in March 2025 was arrested by ICE despite having legal resident status. His wife was pregnant at the time and has since given birth to their child—whom Khalil met in ICE detention. The arrest was widely decried as meant to chill political speech, including by voices not particularly friendly to the pro-Palestine protests. Even as Trump clutches at every lever of power to drive the US toward overt fascism, his ham-fisted tactics and naked egotism create and solidify resistance.

One of the organizers of the film screening mentioned that other area theaters had refused to show the documentary. Yet the theater was nearly filled with sympathetic viewers who wore keffiyehs, hissed at the Columbia president Minouche Shafik, and clapped at the film's end. This highlights something curious about American political discourse right now: it is often hard to tell what the public really thinks about issues, between the enforced hush of mainstream media venues and the clamor in algorithmic echo chambers. Even the New York Times buries news of Palestinians repeatedly massacred at aid distribution sites below the fold, the Instagram feeds of those sympathetic to Palestine are filled with little else. Where do most people really stand?

Increasingly, perhaps they stand together: against an ICE raid in Worcester; against an Israeli weapons company in Cambridge, Massachusetts; against Cop Cities around the country; and even in less-than-half-joking support of Luigi Mangione, the alleged assassin of a health insurance CEO. Official voices cluck about civility and the uselessness of violence while harping on symbolic "resistance" from professional politicians, but more and more ordinary Americans seem to perceive the existing state of violence—which Trump threatens to exacerbate, though it predates him—and are sympathetic to anyone concretely working against it. Looking back at the articles, I was reminded that when voices and votes were actually counted, among citizens of Atlanta and MIT's student body, a clear majority stood against state violence, whether in the form of an expensive police training center or a university working hand in hand with a genocidal military. I was also reminded of a statistic that always gives me hope: 54%, the number of Americans who felt the burning of a Minneapolis police precinct was fully or partially justified in the wake of George Floyd's murder. There's room to work there.

After the film was shown, a panel of pro-Palestinian student activists from Emerson College, MIT, and Harvard answered questions. They reaffirmed their commitment to struggle and pointed to the tasks at hand, such as confronting the conglomerate Maersk over shipments of military supplies to Israel. One student said, "You're seeing the merging of the campus and city activists, and the labor movement is getting involved, too." In his view, the struggles for a free Palestine, for racial justice at home, and for workers are converging. I draw hope from such coalitional thinking: as campus activists like Zeno connected Palestine to campus military contracts, to domestic policing, and to veterans left unhoused; as the fight against Cop City connected environmentalism to the fight for Black lives. We'll need to see our struggles as common in order to save the commons, wherever we claim it, from the quad to the streets to the forest.

At the screening, by the way, I saw a student whom I had interviewed at an encampment last year. They had graduated from law school and are working now as a public defender. I'm glad; the public needs all the defenders it can get.

Walter Smelt III lives in Massachusetts and teaches writing and humanities for local colleges. He holds a master's degree in creative writing from the University of Florida and another in religion, literature, and culture from Harvard Divinity School. His poems have appeared in *Colorado Review, Subtropics, Poetry East,* and *Redivider.*